MENDING BROKEN HEARTS,
REBUILDING SHATTERED LIVES

Mending broken hearts, rebuilding shattered lives

QUAKER PEACEBUILDING IN EAST AND CENTRAL AFRICA

THE 2016 SWARTHMORE LECTURE

ESTHER MOMBO AND CÉCILE NYIRAMANA

First published July 2016

Quaker Books, Friends House, 173 Euston Road, London NW1 2BJ

www.quaker.org.uk

ISBN: 978 1 907123 95 5
eISBN: 978 1 907123 96 2

Book designed and typeset by Cox Design, Witney

Printed by RAP Spiderweb, Oldham

Cover image: Steffen Foerster / Shutterstock.com

THE SWARTHMORE LECTURE

The Swarthmore lectureship was established by the Woodbrooke Extension Committee at a meeting held 9 December 1907. The minute of the committee provided for an "annual lecture on some subject relating to the message and work of the Society of Friends".

The name Swarthmore was chosen in memory of the home of Margaret Fell (later Fox), which was always open to the earnest seeker after Truth, and from which Quakers were sent loving words of sympathy as well as substantial material help.

The lecture is funded by Woodbrooke Quaker Study Centre and overseen and supported by the Swarthmore Lecture Committee, which is appointed by the trustees of Woodbrooke. It is a significant part of the education work undertaken at and from Woodbrooke. The lectureship has a twofold purpose: firstly, to interpret to the members of the Society of Friends their message and mission; and secondly, to bring before the public the spirit, aims and fundamental principles of Friends. The lecturers alone are responsible for any opinions expressed.

The lectureship provides both for the delivery of a lecture, usually at the time of Britain Yearly Meeting of the Society of Friends, and for its dissemination, usually in the form of a book. A lecture related to this publication was delivered at Yearly Meeting in London on the evening of Saturday 28 May 2016.

The Swarthmore Lecture Committee can be contacted via the Clerk, c/o Woodbrooke Quaker Study Centre, 1046 Bristol Road, Selly Oak, Birmingham B29 6LJ.

www.woodbrooke.org.uk/swarthmorelecture

CONTENTS

ACKNOWLEDGEMENTS

The Swarthmore Lecture Committee would like to thank the following, without whom this lecture would not have been possible:

Churchill Malimo, General Secretary, Africa Section of
Friends World Committee for Consultation

David Bucura, former Clerk, Africa Section of
Friends World Committee for Consultation

Gretchen Castle, General Secretary,
Friends World Committee for Consultation

Helen Drewery, General Secretary,
Quaker Peace & Social Witness

Laura Shipler-Chico, Peacebuilding in East Africa
Programme Manager, Quaker Peace & Social Witness

Harry Albright and Ann Floyd, who acted as liaison Friends
to Esther and Cécile in the preparation of the lecture

Staff at Woodbrooke Quaker Study Centre, Birmingham,
and Friends House, London

The William A. Cadbury Charitable Trust and those
Friends and meetings that gave so generously to the fundraising
appeal for the extra costs associated with this lecture.

We also thank the many others who have contributed time, support
and prayers, and of course Esther Mombo and Cécile Nyiramana
for their ministry, which this lecture reflects.

INTRODUCTION

Our names are Esther Mombo and Cécile Nyiramana. In this lecture we are going to try to give you a flavour of Quaker peacebuilding work in five countries in East and Central Africa – Burundi, Democratic Republic of Congo, Kenya, Rwanda, and Uganda. Over the past 20 years these countries have experienced internal conflicts. These have differed from country to country in their severity and their length, and some are still ongoing. Burundi is a case in point, and as we speak towards the end of May 2016 we know that there is fighting in that country, with many people displaced.

We Quakers have been directly affected, and have been challenged to respond. We believe we have made a difference, along with others. There have been some inspiring leaders among us, and we are going to tell you some of their stories.

We have drawn on peacebuilding tools that were already in existence, and have developed some of our own, and we will tell you something about these.

We can also see several general themes in this work, which seem to us to be applicable far beyond our countries, and perhaps to you. We believe you invited us to give this lecture not only to inform yourselves but also because you can see some of the same themes in your own context, and we hope that some of what we will say will speak to your concerns as well.

Our motivation for engaging in peace comes from our personal experiences and also our conviction as Christians following the teachings of Jesus Christ on peace.

Esther: When I was a young woman my grandmother talked to me about Quakers and peace. She told me that Quakers are people who are not engaged in war. She spoke about how her husband was conscripted to war and died in war. He was taken and told he would not be engaged in war but in support of the wounded, but she said it was still against Quaker ideals to participate in war. During the clashes surrounding the 2007 Kenyan election, my brother and family lost everything because my brother was living in a place that was not within his tribe. After a long wait in a police station, he found his way to a safe place. Losing everything meant his children initially could not go to school and as a family we had to see that his children went to school. I experienced what lack of peace meant as we dealt with my brother's shock. Being affected encouraged me to become engaged with peace initiatives in the region.

Cécile: My involvement in peace work comes from my experience of the 1994 genocide against Tutsi in Rwanda. I grew up in a good family, with my brothers and my sisters. When pursuing my studies at university, I met my future husband, and we decided to get married. Then the genocide came and destroyed so many lives and broke so many relationships between Rwandans, who used to be one people. Personally, I lost relatives, friends and my mother. The genocide had incredible consequences; there were many widows and orphans, and many properties were destroyed. In addition, there were many separated families, in which most of the husbands had been arrested and imprisoned and the others had fled the country. Trauma, suspicion, broken hearts, and fractured relationships were the major issues. Then Rwanda Yearly Meeting started a relief programme. Subsequently, in 1998, it began conflict management and healing programmes. I was among the first group to see the light shining in the darkness. Then, as a mother whose husband is still in prison and who had lost family members, I was inspired to do something. I was pushed by the hardship I suffered to heal my broken heart and rebuild relationships for the sake of creating common ground and a safe space for the future of our children. This is why I initiated groups to engage women in dialogue, which bring together widows, genocide survivors and prisoners' wives to work towards reconciliation. I have been doing this ever since 2001. Peacebuilding is my passion.

As well as our personal experiences, the motivation for peace is rooted in Quaker belief in the dignity and worth of all human beings because they are created in the image of God. As such, it is not the will of God for people to be oppressed by poverty, hunger, disease, or tyranny. It is not God's will that people in Africa should be the victims of repression or injustice. God desires the peace and prosperity of all. The social conditions prevailing in East and Central Africa are a major hindrance to the gospel of Jesus Christ. Peacemaking is promoting the activities that will render peace possible, feasible and practicable. Peacemaking is removing the obstacles that prevent peace from being realised.

We'll begin with a quick picture of Quakerism in our countries, to set the scene.

CHAPTER I

Quakerism in East and Central Africa

It is important to note two things from the outset. The first is that about half the Quakers in the world are in Africa. Most are in East and Central Africa, from where we come and the focus of this lecture, though there are small numbers in Southern and West Africa too. The majority of Friends in our region are in Kenya, which has 23 yearly meetings. Burundi and Uganda have two yearly meetings each. Democratic Republic of Congo (DRC), Rwanda and Tanzania have one each. The estimated number of Friends in the region is 600,000.

Secondly, in Africa the different Quaker traditions of unprogrammed, programmed, Evangelical, and Conservative meetings converge. There is one unprogrammed meeting in Nairobi but the majority of meetings in East and Central Africa are programmed or Evangelical. Programmed meetings are aligned to the Friends United Meeting and Evangelical meetings to the Evangelical Friends Church International, both headquartered in the United States. Both the programmed and Evangelical Quaker meetings in Africa emphasise the centrality of Christ and obedience to the teachings of Scripture, and the meetings employ pastors. All the Quaker meetings gather together in the Africa Section of the Friends World Committee for Consultation. It has regional headquarters in Nairobi.

The first Quakers in East Africa settled on Pemba Island and worked with freed slaves. They were followed by American missionaries from Indiana, who arrived in Kenya, which was a British colony, in 1902. Burundi, DRC and Rwanda were Belgian colonies; Tanzania was a German colony; and Uganda was soon to become a British protectorate.

The British colonial government permitted American Quakers Arthur Chilson, Edgar Hole and Willis Hotchkiss to establish a mission station in Kaimosi, in western Kenya. Over the next 60 years the number of Quakers grew substantially, and schools and hospitals were established. Friends Theological College was established in 1942 to train pastors to work in the growing Quaker communities. Among the first women students at the college was Rasoah Mutua, who became a key preacher and a leader of women in Kenya.

Through mission activity by American and African Friends,

Quakerism spread to other countries in East and Central Africa, the largest concentrations being in Burundi and Rwanda. The Quaker meeting in Burundi was founded in 1934 under the guidance of Arthur and Edna Chilson, who had left Kenya in 1927. From Burundi the Quaker church was established in Rwanda by George Morris and Doris and Willard Fergusson, former missionaries to Burundi. The Evangelical Friends Church of Rwanda (Eglise Evangelique des Amis au Rwanda) was founded in 1986. The Free Methodist Church gave these missionaries legal coverage as they applied for the church's legal status. On 13 October 1987 the Evangelical Friends Church of Rwanda was given legal status and many people saw this as a miracle. Missionaries assumed the main leadership positions at first but they soon handed over to the Africans. The distinctive feature of Quakerism in Rwanda is the practice of water baptism. The Quaker church in DRC was founded in 1981 by missionaries from Burundi.

The Quaker meetings in Tanzania were founded by Kenyan Friends who migrated there. Quakers settled on the margins of the Serengeti game reserve. As well as obtaining land, they founded the first Quaker meetings, which were later supported by the then East Africa Yearly Meeting. These meetings grew to become the Tanzania Yearly Meeting in 1980.

The Quaker presence in Uganda also began with Friends from Kenya, and Uganda Yearly Meeting was founded in 1980.

It is significant that the first 50 or 60 years of Quakerism in East and Central Africa were the final years of the colonial period. The process of colonialism varied between countries, but it often exacerbated ethnic tensions such as those between Kikuyu and other tribes in Kenya, and between Hutu and Tutsi in Rwanda and Burundi. These tensions have remained aspects that Africans have had to deal with in relation to peacebuilding. Conflict and violence characterise most of the continent, and East and Central Africa is no exception. For some time now, ethnic-related violent political conflicts have been experienced in five countries where Quakerism is a part of the Christian tradition: Burundi, DRC, Kenya, Rwanda, and Uganda. Tanzania is the exception.

From the 1950s to the 1990s, Rwanda came into the international spotlight for a host of reasons, including ongoing conflicts, a record of severe human rights abuses, and the actions of successive governments that seriously violated the rights of citizens with impunity. Ethnic divisions were further enforced through the enacting and implementation of dehumanising laws and policies, inequality of treatment, and differential access to amenities, basic services and the protection of the state. As a result, many Rwandans left the country as refugees, settling in neighbouring states and further abroad. In 1990 the Rwandese Patriotic Front, based in Uganda, began a war against the Rwandan government in the capital city, Kigali. This caused political instability, higher levels of poverty, infrastructure destruction, and the internal displacement of people. In 1994 an estimated 800,000 Tutsi and moderate Hutu were killed and two million refugees fled the country in one of the most brutal genocides of the twentieth century.

In 1995 the United Nations called for an outreach programme to help prevent future acts of genocide. The Day of Remembrance of the Victims of the Rwanda Genocide has been observed in April each year since 2004, which was ten years after the genocide took place.

Many people around the world hold memorial ceremonies that include candle-lighting and a minute of silence to honour the victims of the Rwanda genocide. This UN day is also a time for diplomats and key community figures to talk with communities about the atrocities of genocide and the importance of working towards a peaceful way of life. Student conferences, exhibitions and other commemorative activities are also held.

Burundi has experienced intermittent internal conflict for many years, and this has recently begun again, after a period of relative calm. As we give this lecture in May 2016, the situation is volatile, with many people displaced and some dead. Dialogue does not appear to be making any headway.

In northern Uganda the conflict in the Acholi district caused by the Lord's Resistance Army began in the 1980s. Many were killed, and many children were kidnapped and forced to become domestic slaves or child soldiers. The aftermath of this continues, with many traumatised people needing ongoing support, as we shall be showing in the testimony of Grace Kiconco later in this lecture.

On the whole, Kenya has been a relatively peaceful space, but the 2007–8 post-election violence threatened this profoundly. Within a few days more than 1,000 people had been killed and over 600,000 rendered homeless, while a significant number were forced to flee their homes and became internally displaced people. The issues behind this conflict were to do with ethnicity, national identity and economic disadvantage.

In all these countries, in recent years, many Friends have responded with peacebuilding initiatives. Until these various conflicts erupted, we, like many Friends around the world, had been living peaceful lives, helping each other and our neighbours in various ways without drawing much attention to ourselves. But some of us have been forced out of our comfort zones and been called to do much more.

We have interpreted peacebuilding very broadly, since as Christians we recognise that peace is not simply the absence of war. It has to do with justice, reconciliation, healing, and forgiveness. Quakers in the region have engaged in various forms of peacebuilding. Some of us have worked to resolve conflicts, and some of us have focused on post-conflict trauma-healing and rehabilitation. Some of us have worked to ameliorate the conditions that give rise to conflict, by meeting basic needs such as food and shelter. Some of us have worked to make society function more equitably, for example through nonviolent campaigns aimed at reducing discrimination, by developing peace education, or through election-monitoring and developing civic skills. Creating work opportunities, especially for young people and women, has been another strand.

An important aim of our peacebuilding has been to help communities to heal and be reconciled to each other so that they grow together as communities. Violence causes segregation along identity lines, with individuals and groups becoming isolated and exclusive, claiming that they are only safe "when with my people". As Quakers we embark on peacebuilding to help reconcile people to God, to their neighbours and to nature. Our work begins with dealing with the hurt at the individual level, and also healing at all levels of society for lasting peace. We do this because conflict in our region is rooted in a politics of exclusion in which people find themselves denied their identity, freedom or resources. As a result people react. Change or transformation of the pain stems from faith. If healing is to bring people and communities together across cultures, the first step is forgiveness. Reconciliation therefore means creating new relationships, and this begins with healing past hurts and framing a vision for a better future.

It is against this background that several diverse means have been used in peacebuilding in the region. We will now describe some of the tools we have used, along with examples of situations where they have been helpful.

CHAPTER 2

Peacebuilding tools

Conflict management

In conflict management workshops we teach individuals and organisations skills for dealing with interpersonal disputes without the aid of a neutral third party. Trainees learn both how to negotiate with others to create more durable and meaningful resolutions and how to communicate more effectively with others in order to decrease instances of disputes in the first place.

Conflict management workshops have been used in Rwanda since 1998. They were introduced by the Mennonite Central Committee in the aftermath of the genocide. This has helped to reduce the number of disputes as well as helping the two ethnic sides to deal with disputes themselves. Since then Friends Peace House has received many requests from the community to help people learn basic conflict management skills.

Mediation

Mediation involves a neutral third party in resolving disputes. Though many community leaders have received and are using basic skills in conflict management, there are still many cases requiring mediation in communities in Rwanda (and elsewhere) where relationships have been broken by the atrocities of the 1994 genocide. The basic five-day mediation training course is based on a programme developed by an organisation called Change Agents for Peace International; it lays the groundwork for anyone interested in becoming a mediator. In Rwanda some of those trained go on to become volunteer mediators with Friends Peace House.

This tool has been used successfully to mediate between survivors and offenders from both ethnic groups in Rwanda. It has also been taught in Quaker primary and secondary schools to reduce conflicts between students, teachers and parents' committees. It has contributed a lot to promoting the culture of peace in Quaker schools.

It has been used extensively in Burundi too. One Burundian peaceworker told us:

I am Levi Ndikumana, founder of Ministry for Peace and Reconciliation under the Cross (MIPAREC) and the national coordinator of the peacemaking project Sangwamahoro in Burundi. My country has been ravaged by violent ethnic conflict since 1993. There were two options for young people: join the armed groups or go for peacebuilding. Since then, MIPAREC has contributed to peacebuilding by equipping young people with conflict management and mediation skills. Many peace committees have been born, and they have been able to mediate within communities. They have successfully brought together people from different ethnic groups using the tools of conflict management and mediation.

Alternatives to Violence Project

Providing conflict management and mediation skills to bring together two parties in conflict has not been enough in many communities in Burundi, Democratic Republic of Congo (DRC), Kenya, and Rwanda. There are pressing needs to work on the prevention of conflict by promoting the culture of nonviolence. This is why the Alternatives to Violence Project (AVP) has been another valuable tool for us. It was brought to us by Friends from the United States, through the African Great Lakes Initiative, usually known as AGLI.

AVP began in 1975, when a group of prison inmates near New York City asked a local Quaker group to provide them with nonviolence training. Highly experiential in nature, the workshops encourage participants to recognise that they can best find their *own* answers to the conflicts they encounter, without resorting to violence. AVP workshops focus on seeking that which is good in ourselves and others, and on cooperation, community-building skills, trust, respect, and inclusiveness. They foster communication skills, deep listening, speaking with clarity, and responsibility – all leading to conflict transformation.

There are three levels of AVP training: Basic, Advanced and Training for Facilitators. All workshops last for three days and emphasise building community among participants. The Basic workshop provides an initial introduction to the concepts outlined. In the Advanced workshop, participants choose the thematic focus that they want to explore more fully. Examples of such themes include fear, anger, forgiveness, and discrimination. In the Training for Facilitators workshop, participants learn the skills needed to lead workshops on their own.

AGLI introduced AVP to Rwanda in 2001, Burundi in 2002, western Kenya and Nairobi in 2003, and eastern Congo in 2005. These programmes now all have local experienced, trained AVP facilitators and lead facilitators who can offer Advanced workshops and Training for Facilitators workshops. AVP is now also being used as basic training for specific peace work in the region when funding is available: for example, with youth in Kenya who experienced the post-election violence of 2007–8 and with returned Hutu and Tutsi refugees from Tanzania who have been resettled in Rwanda.

AVP teaches people that they can choose to respond to violence using active nonviolence. This tool has helped prisoners, grassroots leaders, local government, and many Gacaca judges in Rwanda. In Rwandan tradition, *gacaca* (a word meaning "justice amongst the grass") is a communal justice method that was adapted in 2001 following the 1994 genocide. The genocide led to the deaths, torture and rape of an estimated 800,000 people and there was a need to develop an effective way to detain and try the more than 100,000 people accused of genocide and war crimes. It was estimated that it would take more than 100 years to try such a massive number of accused using the existing justice methods. The solution was to adapt the *gacaca* system to work in concert with the International Criminal Tribunal for Rwanda, to ensure that justice was speedy but also fair.

Though the Gacaca judges had been trained, it became clear that they needed peacebuilding skills. That's why Friends Peace House recommended that AVP be used to build the judges' capacity to seek that which is good in others, and to work on cooperation and on building trust, respect and inclusiveness. The judges also learnt communication skills. This was in Western Province, Ngoma District, and AVP equipped the judges as well as community leaders with new skills, as mentioned in the following testimony:

I am Sizeli Marcellin from Rwanda Friends Peace House. I remember when we organised AVP training for the community leaders from Ngoma District. The vice mayor of good governance told us that AVP is a tremendous tool for good governance: "The skills we have now will help us to respond peacefully in a situation of violence. They will also help us leaders to treat peacefully those who come to us. We will be able to listen to them and understand them, and will be able to find ways to solve their problems. We are grateful for this important tool for peace."

AVP is also helping prisoners in Rwanda. Most of them say that they never before realised that there is an option to respond to violence with nonviolence. If they had benefitted from AVP before the genocide, they would not be in prison. They are promising to use AVP principles in prison and among their families as well as in their respective communities when out of prison.

Healing and Rebuilding Our Communities

One major consequence of tribal and ethnic conflict in Africa is deeply wounded and broken hearts. It would be impossible to reconcile communities without considering the unhealed wounds and the deep traumas many have experienced. This is why a new tool was developed in Burundi and Rwanda, working with AGLI: Healing and Rebuilding Our Communities (HROC).

This programme takes ten people from one side of a conflict and ten people from the other side on a three-day workshop to restore the relationships between the two sides. In Rwanda, this means Tutsi survivors of the genocide and the families of Hutu perpetrators of the genocide. In Burundi, this also means ten Tutsi and ten Hutu in each workshop.

The HROC programme is based on a set of key principles and assumptions. Firstly, the HROC programme believes that in every person there is something good. This is a radical notion in societies where most members have witnessed neighbours and even family members committing gruesome acts of violence.

Secondly, the programme is based on the belief that each person and each society has the inner capacity to heal, and an inherent intuition regarding how to recover from trauma. Healing from trauma requires that a person's inner good and wisdom are sought and shared with others. It is through this effort that trust can begin to be restored.

Thirdly, HROC understands that both victims and perpetrators of violence experience trauma and its after-effects.

Fourthly, the violence in Burundi and Rwanda was experienced at both a personal and a community level. Therefore, efforts to heal and rebuild each country must also happen at both the individual and the community level.

Lastly, healing from trauma and building peace between groups are deeply connected; it is not possible to do one successfully without the other. Trauma-healing and peacebuilding efforts must happen simultaneously.

The HROC programme slowly builds trust within a group. It is common for participants to be wary of attending workshops, fearing they might be a trap where they will be attacked, sent back to prison or killed. Through experiential activities and cooperative exercises, participants begin to relax. Ground rules are set to increase the "Sense of Safety", the first stage.

The second stage is "Remembrance and Mourning". There are two Rwandan proverbs that emphasise the importance of speaking out about one's pain: "the family that does not talk, dies" and "the man who is sick must tell the whole world". Traditionally, Burundians and Rwandans talk about their losses and talk through their grief with family and neighbours. Broken trust and dismantled families have impeded that intuitive process of healing, but it is widely accepted in the cultures there as an important step in the journey towards healing.

In the workshops a forum is created for participants to pay tribute to their losses and to share their grief with others. This process helps to humanise the "other", thereby laying the foundation for the third and final stage, "Reconnection". Many programme participants report having felt very isolated in their grief and their reactions to the trauma they have experienced. The workshops become an important first step in realising that they are not alone. Those who seek the second level of training – to become peer counsellors – begin to see how they can use their own painful experiences to help others. As one recent participant, a genocide orphan, wrote in her evaluation:

> I was thinking that I have nothing in me, but I found that I can even use my wounds to heal other people and I found that there is a good thing in every person, even though that person is full of trauma and problems.

Another important aspect of reconnection is the process of rebuilding relationships across the lines of "Hutu" and "Tutsi", thereby strengthening the fabric of communities torn apart by a long history of violence. The testimony of one participant illustrates this:

> I am Solange Maniraguha from HROC Rwanda. Firstly, HROC helped me to heal my heart's wounds. It is not easy for a broken-hearted healer to listen to someone who is traumatised. But what I like about HROC is that it is helping people to discover themselves, to recognise their wickedness and trauma, to rehabilitate themselves, and then try to help those who are in need of healing. In addition, HROC helps to heal wounded hearts, encouraging people to forgive each other and then be reconciled. For example, in the community of Gisenyi, two families reconciled successfully. One survivor and a released prisoner who attended HROC training decided to forgive each other and their families became real friends. They are helping more people in forgiveness and reconciliation.

And here is another testimony, from Grace Kiconco from northern Uganda, concerning work with child soldiers who had been forced to serve in the Lord's Resistance Army, and also with their victims:

Through my involvement with soldiers, I found they were fearing and anxious. They were just like the victims. I realised that what the government would say or what the rest of Ugandans would say about child soldiers or their victims was different from the real experiences that the people were having. And later we did some work managing anger and a lot of the people, even those who didn't read or write, were able to express themselves, their anger about the things that had happened to them during the war. And so much was related not just to the experience then. A lot of them went very far back in their lives, to their childhoods. So connecting to people's real lives more and more gave me the impetus to continue in this work.

Much later, in 2013 or 2014, I started doing the HROC work, again in northern Uganda, with people from the Lord's Resistance Army war. I wouldn't know how to describe it because there were times you would get in a room and somebody would tell their story and start screaming and crying. And I would think, how are we going to manage? We only have three days. People are screaming. They are showing there is a lot of pain. Are we just going to leave them with open wounds? But that short time rebuilding community, having people share together, seeing that there are other people with pain – it allowed healing to take place.

Friends are among the people in this world who are still doing great work, who still believe in not necessarily publicising themselves but working from their hearts and continuing with whatever group of people it is, whether poor or rich, in their simple way doing great things, extraordinary things.

Entrepreneurship, saving and credit programmes

We know that addressing the root causes of conflict is better than dealing with the consequences of conflict. Poverty is one hindrance to sustainable peace, so some of those working on peacebuilding in Burundi, DRC, Kenya, and Rwanda have addressed poverty. They have used a new tool, training people in entrepreneurship and setting up saving and credit programmes to reduce poverty, including micro-credit schemes. This tool is used to change the mindset of the community in terms of economic empowerment, to open up their eyes to what they can do, to provide sources of start-up capital, and to show them how they can work together to generate an income to improve the standard of life of their families.

Economic empowerment contributes a lot to the sustainability of the peace work. For instance, in the community of Bugesera in Rwanda, survivors and released prisoners have been trained in AVP and HROC, and now construct houses together. They stay together, living in the same neighbourhood, and have been reconciled and have forgiven each other. Now they are still working together to share in the country a message of forgiveness and reconciliation.

Turning the Tide

Turning the Tide (TTT) is a social action training programme developed by Britain Yearly Meeting's Quaker Peace & Social Witness (QPSW). It aims to advance the understanding and practice of active nonviolence to 'turn the tide' of injustice, oppression and disempowerment and to build a just and peaceful world. Turning the Tide describes nonviolence as "a way of actively confronting injustice. Not doing nothing, not responding violently, not running away; but struggling creatively to transform the situation. It's about doing conflict better; bringing about change without doing harm."[1]

The core principles of Turning the Tide are as follows:
- a willingness to take action to resist injustice
- to act in ways that appeal to the humanity in our opponent
- to respect and care for everyone involved, including our opponent
- a refusal to harm, damage or degrade people, the environment or living things
- if suffering is inevitable, a willingness to take it on yourself rather than inflict it on others

1 Turning the Tide offers workshops, courses and resources to groups working for nonviolent social change. Find out more at www.turningtide.org.uk.

- a belief that everyone is capable of change
- to recognise that no one has a monopoly on truth, so we aim to bring together our 'truth' and the opponents' 'truth'
- an understanding that the means shape the ends, so the methods we use have to be consistent with the ends of justice and peace that we seek
- a recognition of the importance of training so that we continually learn and practise nonviolence.

Turning the Tide began working in Kenya in 2009 in partnership with AGLI and Change Agents for Peace International to support local campaigners to stand up for human rights and social justice using the skills of active nonviolence. This pilot project adapted Turning the Tide's approach to the Kenyan context and led to a fully fledged programme that is locally driven and relies largely on community-based volunteers and trainers. This current work is supported by the Peacebuilding in East Africa Programme of QPSW.

Turning the Tide has been extended to Rwanda in partnership with Rwanda Yearly Meeting and to Burundi in partnership with the Ministry for Peace and Reconciliation under the Cross (MIPAREC) to empower local peace activists to make their voices heard while advocating for human rights promotion as well as social justice. Here is an example from Rwanda:

I am Daniel Nteziyaremye, one of the TTT workers. In Rubavu District, Western Province, the community-based nonviolence campaigns identified a case of injustice against an orphan of about 17 years old who had been raped. She got pregnant and the family decided to keep quiet. Her stepfather and the perpetrator decided to imprison her in a family room until they had found a way to abort her pregnancy. The TTT resource people mobilised the community, spoke about the case and learned about further injustices that had happened to the orphan. They then decided to work with the local governance leaders to plead and advocate for the girl. Then, together with the community leaders, they came to talk to the girl's family and asked them to free her from the prison where they had put her. They then took the girl to the hospital and reported the case to the police. Now the orphan has a beautiful baby girl, though she is traumatised by what she went through. In addition, she is being followed up by the counsellors, who are helping her to recover. She is very thankful to TTT, which advocated for her and helped her to find justice. Unfortunately, the two men – her stepfather and the perpetrator – fled the country to DRC. The community and the girl's family salute the work of TTT in Rubavu.

Using these tools

All of these tools have been translated into local languages to make them domesticated and more effective. They can also be adapted to meet the needs of the community concerned.

The tools do not have to be used on their own. From our own experience, they can often be used together in the same community to great advantage: there is often a greater impact than when using only one because this can address the consequences of war or violent conflict more holistically.

For example, we realised that when we used only AVP in one community or only trauma-healing in another community, both were helpful, but not enough to bring about real change.

However, when we took AVP, trauma-healing, conflict resolution, and entrepreneurship, saving and credit as a package to the same community, this resulted in much more impact and change. This happened in Musanze among a group of women in dialogue, who went through the healing process, obtained skills on alternatives to violence, and learned about conflict resolution and prevention. Then we gave them skills in entrepreneurship and supported their peace networks. Today, the groups are still working together on peace and development.

Sometimes people adapt one tool to include others, as a Burundian Friend says:

> I am David Niyonzima from Trauma Healing and Reconciliation Services Burundi. I am using AVP as an approach because I found that it brings together the healing model, the prevention of violence and the transformation of the conflict.

CHAPTER 3

Emerging themes

Addressing root causes

From the various methodologies that have been mentioned and from the testimonies of the people we have heard, we know that peacemakers in East and Central Africa are engaged in dealing with various root causes of conflict and violence. In situations of conflict, peacebuilders have always dealt first of all with the immediate needs of those who are affected. But once that has been done, reconciliation and rebuilding are vital so that shattered lives can be rebuilt.

In the Kenyan situation during the post-election violence of 2007–8, people in most parts of the Rift Valley were displaced and forced to live in camps after their homes were burnt down. Discussing Friends' response, Joseph Mamai, who was then the presiding clerk of Friends Church Peace Teams, said:

> We came together and asked ourselves what we could do as a peace church. The first thing we did was to attend to the physical needs of the people affected before we began looking into other needs. After dealing with the physical needs, we knew that these people could not live in tents; they had to return to their homes – but their homes had been destroyed. The government decreed that all the people should return to their farms. But, listening to the people in the camps, I learnt that they were not ready to return and the others in the villages were not ready to receive them.
>
> One of the issues was the new identities that people had acquired – namely, "perpetrators" and "victims". This language was intimidating and was creating more animosity between the two groups, so we chose new words. We called those who had done the evicting the "receiving group" and those who had been evicted the "returning people". We set a day to meet the people in each of the camps and together discussed the mode of returning and the ways in which the returning group would be received. After days of discussion the two groups agreed that the evictees would return and be received. The receiving group accommodated the returnees and helped them to rebuild their houses.

The root causes of conflict in our region include a destructive style of ethnicity, denominationalism, political and economic leadership, a frustrated democratisation process, inadequate international cooperation, corruption, and poverty, to name but a few. These causes are both internal and external and are both historical and contemporary. Kenya well illustrates these root causes.

In Kenya the boundaries have remained the same in postcolonial times as they were in colonial times. These colonial boundaries reflected both ethnic and denominational segregation. For instance, the Presbyterian Church of East Africa was established in Central Province and is ethnically identified with Kikuyu. The African Inland Mission is in the Rift Valley and is associated with the Kalenjin community. The Quakers, originally established in Western Province, are identified with some of the Luhya dialects: Bukusu, Isukha, Maragoli, and Tiriki. This ethnic and denominational segregation feeds into negative and power politics when politicians capitalise on exclusion and marginalisation. The "us and them" political syndrome that brings about divisions based on a negative view of the other encourages animosity and lack of trust of the other. The other's image is portrayed as that which will take over and rule in a terrible way. The other is portrayed as one who will not share resources; the other is portrayed as evil. In this situation the youth are manipulated and used to fight each other rather than being encouraged to ask questions of the politicians about what structural plans they have for enhancing growth.

When peacebuilders address the root causes of these issues, they can help people to better understand the dynamics of conflict. In doing this, one does not shy away from naming the historical grievances around cultural ethnic tensions that continue to rock communities. In addressing the legacies of historical injustice, peacebuilders are engaged in deeper dialogue about recurring intergroup tensions and are rebuilding trust.

Leadership

The quality of leadership is one such root cause. During her Nobel Peace Prize acceptance speech in Oslo on 10 December 2004,

Kenyan Wangari Maathai said:

> I call on leaders, especially from Africa, to expand democratic space and build fair and just societies that allow the creativity and energy of their citizens to flourish.
>
> Those of us who have been privileged to receive education, skills, and experiences and even power must be role models for the next generation of leadership.[2]

The challenge that Maathai raised is not uniquely African; there are other places in the world with similar issues. Since we are talking about one region where Quakers are engaged in peacebuilding, we will illustrate it from that angle.

Our region has been through various constitutional changes, each of which has amended the period of time politicians can stay in power. The terms vary but one of the root causes of conflict is individuals staying in leadership positions for long periods. This creates fear and deters growth and healthy opposition.

The cycle of poor and/or bad leadership helps to cause election violence, as propaganda, fear and intimidation are used to silence any voices that are contrary to the voice of those in power. We can conclude that lack of good governance contributes to many of the conflicts in our society today. In addition, the obstacles to the achievement and the maintenance of peace and good governance across the region are embedded in patriarchy, as exhibited in practices that thrive on discrimination and exclusion on the basis of age, gender, ethnicity, and/or religion. The Christian church is not free of these problems internally and neither are Quakers. In peacebuilding, it is safe to begin by using the various methodologies tried and tested among Quakers. Within this tradition, people are able to address difficult issues, often avoided, that cause recurrent tension or prohibit healing. Free from outside judgement, the use of familiar language and history for self-critique and constructive inner work is a source and example of peace work.

---

2   Wangari Maathai, 'Nobel lecture', www.nobelprize.org/nobel_prizes/peace/laureates/ 2004/maathai-lecture-text.html, accessed 18 April 2016. © The Nobel Foundation

Poor sharing of natural resources

In discussing peacebuilding, one cannot avoid the issue of reconciliation to God, neighbour and environment. In our work we have discovered that poor sharing of natural resources breeds tension and conflict. The election of leaders is based on how the natural resources will be divided and what one region will get over another in a given context.

In places such as Democratic Republic of Congo (DRC), which is rich in minerals that would bring good revenue to the country, conflict and war have made it hard for people to benefit from what is within their reach. Instead, communities are embroiled in conflict while leaders and people from outside benefit from the natural resources. The leadership is capable of stopping the wars and creating governance that supports and benefits all, but it does not do so. While this is viewed as an internal affair, there are external forces in play as well, namely the international community, for which conflict can be advantageous, as conflict can enable it to keep exploiting the natural resources. It is true to say that conflicts in Africa are at times a source of income for various vested interests.

In East and Central Africa there are few or no economic opportunities. The population explosion has produced an educated youth who are frustrated because of unemployment and who lack capital to start up a business. The challenge of urban migration has led to a steady growth of slums where the tensions and frustrations are concentrated. In rural areas, grievances are most pronounced over land access and alienation of land. Most of these grievances are rooted in a sense of ethnic or sectarian marginalisation. These grievances have been easily tapped and sometimes manipulated by political elites.

High levels of poverty create animosity among people, especially when they are electing leaders in either the religious or public spheres. Those who experience poverty can be divided into two categories – the marginalised and the exploited. The marginalised are those who are outside the prevailing economic system and include the unemployed, the homeless, abandoned children, outcasts, the disabled, and the aged. The exploited are those who are treated unjustly by the socio-economic system. Corruption – when people take what is in the public coffers for themselves and their own families – has also been named as a root cause of conflict. The scandal of poverty is real in most of the countries in the region and is another root source of conflict. Each government that is voted into power uses the need to wipe out corruption but fails to do so and is voted out.

So there is a need to work strategically on the political and economic system as a whole, as well as at the grass roots. Both are necessary, if fundamental change is to occur. Quaker peacebuilding work in the region has paid more attention to the grass roots than to the strategic context. However, where grassroots work is extensive, it can often come to the attention of political and other leaders and be adopted by them in some form.

Cécile has personal experience of this. In 2001, when she started to bring together widows, genocide survivors and prisoners' wives, most of her church members told her that it was in vain. But she was committed to furthering the process of reconciliation between those two blocs, which were supposed to be enemies, using tools such as the Alternatives to Violence Project, conflict resolution and Healing and Rebuilding Our Communities (HROC). The women released their anger and sorrow, forgave each other and decided to work together to bring a message of peace and reconciliation. Some of their husbands have confessed, been forgiven, have come back to their families and are living peacefully with the survivors. Today, these groups are serving as a good example of reconciliation in their respective communities. In Gicumbi and Musanze Districts the groups have received an award from the National Commission of Unity and Reconciliation, for working successfully on reconciling relationships.

Sustainability

Another key issue is sustainability, which is closely connected to funding. When people read about peacebuilding, the impression is often given that all peace work is based on donor funding. This may be because some of these projects are big and receive publicity. They create jobs for those who qualify, some of whom are motivated by money. These projects are sustained as long as there is money to run them. This kind of work could be called "project peace". This is the peace work that is recognised and that hits the headlines of the local and international papers. This type of peace work is time-limited and is dependent on the aims of the donor, so it may not be sustainable.

Donor-funded peace work can lead to projects that are not well coordinated and may not meet the most important needs. Donors have their own constraints, which drive what they can fund. Sometimes their funds unwittingly change the distribution of power and authority. Since the donor may not know the local dynamics, the funds can create division among the recipients. Donors may not want to work with the local structures – be they religious or political – and create other structures that may not necessarily help the affected. Donors often require specific ways of reporting, and reports often have to be tailor-made to suit the needs of the donor. Donor-funded projects support the external desire to do something, anything, to help. The ways the funds are raised are all too often dependent on exploiting the images of the people in conflict.

These types of projects can be used to justify and enhance an external agenda. The external agenda may be tied to the political and economic needs of the donor. This may not be to end the conflict but to continue it, because it creates jobs for the external people. Donor funding can also create a situation of dependency such that when the funds stop then peace work stops. It is too often dependent on images and not on a needs analysis. Donor funding at times is used to bandage issues rather than deal with the root causes.

Don't get us wrong. We are grateful for the help and support of individuals and agencies that can bring resources and expertise, working in collaboration with local communities and agencies, helping those communities and agencies to better do the work that they are called to do. These include projects that have been supported by Quakers from Britain, Norway and the United States. Their contributions have helped considerably. For example:

- Friends peace teams through the African Great Lakes Initiative have supported many projects, including many of the HROC programmes.

- American Friends Service Committee has been very supportive of the Quaker Peace Network and of election-monitoring work.
- Quaker Service Norway for many years supported peacebuilding in Burundi, DRC, Kenya, Rwanda, Tanzania, and Uganda through Change Agents for Peace (later Change Agents for Peace International).
- Britain Yearly Meeting's Quaker Peace & Social Witness has supported a lot of peacebuilding in Burundi, DRC, Kenya, and Rwanda. Turning the Tide is one of its very successful programmes, which is bringing about the hoped-for change in Africa.
- Various yearly meetings in Europe (including Britain Yearly Meeting) and the United States are supporting schools and peace centres in Africa.

But a system of peace projects that rely solely on donor money and external agencies is not only dangerous but also unsustainable. Sustainable peacebuilding requires, firstly, a holistic approach to conflict, violence and war. Secondly, it must deal with local politico-economic issues as well as religious, spiritual and ethical issues. Thirdly, the inclusion of all stakeholders, especially women, is vital for sustainable peace.

Sustainable peacebuilding must include the people themselves recognising the importance of initiatives. Often, such recognitions arise from bonds between people based on their faith. When people begin to think critically about how Quakers approach the example and teachings of Jesus and what faith in him requires, they realise that they do not need funding but space to meet with each other. That is why there is an increasing number of churches in East and Central Africa doing peace work without donor funding. This is not peacebuilding done in the abstract. It is inclusive of trauma-healing and is based on hearing and sharing the experiences of each other and knowing that as a people and as individuals we are all wounded. These narratives are a motivation for peace among the people. In this regard the people seek that which can help them to grow in their community and to access facilities. Rather than waiting for donors, the people choose to develop resources that can sustain their work.

These resources include supporting each person to obtain that which they do not have materially. Even where donor funding is sought, the work is based on much ongoing peacebuilding within communities. This work is done, often by women, at various levels – feeding the hungry, clothing the naked, visiting those who are struck by calamity. This spontaneous work on peace is sustainable because it is based on and rooted in community. The motivation for such peace work is based on the belief in the humanity of the other and the teaching of Jesus that "blessed are the peacemakers" (Matthew 5:9). We applaud these groups that make efforts to make peace on every front, be it home, church community or nation at large.

So sustainable peace work is not externally driven but internally driven. It is clear that donor funding is limited and often dries up unless there is further conflict. When communities get tired of conflict and choose to make peace, they risk losing support that they have come to rely upon. It is in this connection that peaceworker Hezron Masitsa observes:

> I wish peace work was not done as a profession because its link with a project is based on money, and this does not come from people's hearts but a job.

For Masitsa and others, peace has become a profession that pays rather than a way of life that helps us to be at peace with each other. Positive peace initiatives are rooted in the needs of the community and have various methods of dealing with issues that bring conflict. They teach people how to avoid violence in the first place, and how to work with each other during or after conflict to bring lasting peace. These initiatives include the various and important methods of dealing with conflict that emanate from the Quaker ethos, including those that we have mentioned, such as AVP, HROC and restorative justice.

Burundian David Niyonzima says:

> The peace work we are doing is sustainable in the sense that the workshops we are doing are a form of training that will be duplicated by the trained ones. What makes these workshops sustainable is the fact that we move from basic training to advanced training, and the skills and life changes are lived out by the workshop attendees in their constituencies.

In this respect, we have found the analysis of Diana Francis helpful. In her book *From pacification to peacebuilding*, she sets out two worldviews on peacebuilding. The first is based on interdependence and the other on the law of the jungle, where one must eat or be eaten:

> As I see it, peacebuilding, as understood within conflict transformation, begins from the worldview in which interdependence is the point of departure, orientating people and institutions towards peacebuilding as cooperation, while the worldview that sees life as a matter of eating or being eaten leads to what I have termed 'pacification'.[3]

If what Francis says is true, then Masitsa's observations are also true. It is dangerous to have a large number of peace networks working independently and financially supported by various organisations, because this leads to serial peace-conference-going, creating desks of peace projects that rival each other and creating reactive spaces instead of proactive spaces in which to deal with conflicts and war. In East and Central Africa some of this has happened and it is unsustainable.

Sustainable peacebuilding requires an approach to conflict, violence and war where people are able to speak about these issues in forums where they feel safe. Peace processes should be able to move from training in safe places for just a few people to being with others in the places where they are hurting. As well as providing spaces in which to discuss conflict, sustainable peace work means

---

3 Diana Francis, *From pacification to peacebuilding: A call to global transformation* (London: Pluto Press, 2010), pp. 73–74.

including in the training all the people within conflict areas, not just dealing with leaders who struggle to share power and often abuse it. Men, women and young people must be included in the training for peace and the naming of the issues that are leading to conflict in their communities. This is the pattern and example that Quakers seek to bring to this work.

Education

Education is an important medium of peacebuilding. It can bring to light root causes and contribute to dealing with those root causes. It is an important contributor to sustainability.

The establishment of Quakerism in East and Central Africa occurred through a fourfold methodology that included evangelism, education, health, and practical services. Education became a medium for creating communities of people who were different from each other in the way they approached issues. At independence most of the new presidents vowed to deal with issues of ignorance through education. In peacebuilding one cannot avoid education as a way of dealing with conflict. Peacebuilding courses have been offered to numerous groups through donor funding, but, as one Rwandan attender observes,

> I have over 25 certificates on peace but they are not recognised in the context of study.

This remark has many implications to it and can be analysed more deeply. However, the education we are talking about in peacebuilding is not one that is undertaken for certificates alone. It is also important that it helps to inculcate in learners the values of peace and models of maintaining peace. Such education is undertaken not only for our own good but also as people of faith, as it is a way of portraying our Christian ethos. As Quakers it is our calling and our mark.

The peacebuilding short courses that are donor-funded target grassroots people who are or have been in conflict zones and who could be victims and/or perpetrators. Sometimes these people do not have any other qualification that can give them status or identity or enable them to analyse conflict dynamics. Education is important and critical for peacebuilding, and any funding process should take this seriously. An educated population is not vulnerable to the whims of politicians who have vested interests in sensitising the masses to vote for them or to join in battles when they lose. Education for peace is not only offered formally in seminars but can also take place in different forums, as in the example of Mama Peace:

One day I was travelling from Kakamega to my home in Kiminini, Kenya. I was in a noisy *matatu* (minibus) and I heard two young men plotting an attack on a village adjacent to my home. The members of this village were from a different ethnic community from the one the young men came from. They were angry with people from this ethnic community because they had settled in their land. The young men saw them as intruders who had become rich from resources that did not belong to them.

I did not like what I heard and I decided to engage the young men in a conversation when the *matatu* stopped and we alighted. I began by acknowledging the fact that they had issues that were real and painful. I invited them to my house and we continued the discussion on their pain and animosity towards their neighbours. I listened to their complaints and in discussion we agreed that attacking this village was not the solution to their grievances but that we could look for another way.

I came to an agreement with these young people that they would not attack this village and I would not tell the police or the villagers about what they had been planning. I became friends with a team of young people and began seeking solutions to their problems of unemployment. I began organising seminars for the young people and creatively looking for ways in which they could be empowered with skills in order to support themselves and their families. Today most of them have joined schemes that have given them work to do and/or business, and they named me Mama Peace.

Mama Peace's real name is Rose Imbega. From the testimony of Rose it is clear that education should be aimed at those who are as vulnerable as these young people were. It is possible that they had been told that their problems had arisen because of the different tribe settling in their community, which was not true. Mama Peace was able to avert the conflict by helping the young people to understand the dynamics of power politics. Together they were able to look for a long-term solution.

The Quaker peacebuilding community has embarked on curriculum development for schools, which, while sponsored by Quakers, admit students from various ethnic communities and denominations, and also from various regions. The context of the post-election violence of 2007–8 awakened Quakers to talk of the Quaker peace ethos in their schools. One element of this was the development of the peace curriculum, which was to be integrated into the school programmes. The tools of AVP and HROC were employed in schools to create a conducive learning atmosphere among students who came from different tribal backgrounds and had been affected by the violence. As well as using these tools to help integrate the students, a draft Charter was developed, setting out the values and strategies that Friends schools should manifest, based on such key themes as peace and nonviolence, truth and integrity, and equality. But the peace education that will be long-lasting is one that is inculcated in the whole educational programme. The responsibility of government is to invest in the education of its people.

This will empower the people in various ways. It will empower people to survive so that people are safeguarded from abuse and destruction. It will empower people to name the issues that are destroying them. This includes naming those that are in the community who abuse people. Many, at times the powerful, mute the voices of the people in the community – and this is not uniquely an African situation; it can take place anywhere.

Education empowers people to live in solidarity and interdependence. This form of empowerment calls for greater awareness of the deep connections between life, the realisation of justice and the redistribution of power in all structures of human relationships. Education for empowerment must also involve questioning and redefining power. It is true that silencing dissent is an ongoing feature of all human relationships at every level. To silence people and to deny them the chance to interrogate and redefine their realities serves the interests of leaders who cannot cope with their own vulnerabilities and feelings of insecurity. Finally, empowering education is education that teaches people to exercise power responsibly.

The important contribution of women

Finally, we'd like to discuss the crucial role women have played in peacebuilding.

In Rwanda, women are leading by example, as you have heard. In Kenya, within Quaker meetings, women have also led by example. The United Society of Friends Women (USFW) in Kenya was formed in 1952 as a separate meeting. USFW has helped women to find space to deliberate on matters that affect them and the community. One of these has been peace and conflict within the Quaker movement and also externally. USFW was crucial in building peace among the yearly meetings, leading to the formation of Friends Church Kenya. When the leaders of the yearly meetings were not talking to each other, women from various yearly meetings started a prayer meeting together. The women met in each other's homes to pray and talk to each other. Some of these women talked to each other even if their husbands who were in leadership were not talking to each other. What started as a prayer meeting of a few women grew into the USFW in Kenya. When the men saw this they began coming together to create Friends Church Kenya.

Women in all parts of Africa continue to struggle for their empowerment in both private and public spaces. Even if some strides have been made in the political, social, economic, and religious spheres of life (for example, in 2015 the first woman clerk was appointed in Bware Yearly Meeting), the situation of exclusion and marginalisation is still the reality. One peaceworker told us:

> While I was busy with peace projects my own mother was among the people excluded and marginalised in a patriarchal system. Restorative justice helped me to look inward and to see how my mother had been abused due to the injustices rooted in the patriarchal culture. My mother tried to fit into a patriarchal cultural system but failed. She was rejected when alive and rejected at death. After she died I had to argue with my uncles on where to bury her; the "crime" she had committed was not to stay within an abusive marriage. I realised that, even though Quakers were historically among the first people to open up space for women, in the Quaker meetings I attended women were still defined from the cultural perspective that they were not allowed into positions of leadership. Denying women space to exercise their gifts was and is a justice issue, and so, when one is dealing with peace and conflict issues, it should start from the relationship between men and women. The Quaker church in Kenya has done many things but should lead by example on all issues, especially in the ways in which women are dealt with.

It is gratifying to note that 50 years of struggle for women's empowerment seems to have started paying off. Many positive results have been achieved, and women's contribution to the church and society has both increased and gained recognition in our times. There have been significant changes in the law about women's employment, inheritance, property ownership, and marriage. We have witnessed changing attitudes towards the education of girls and women, the professional status of women, and the participation of women in leadership and management. Presently, gender-sensitive women and men in Africa continue to call for the empowerment of women and the redressing of gender-based discrimination as we continue to struggle for the establishment of democratic institutions and responsible governance. Nevertheless, despite these laudable strides, a lot remains to be done. Society is still structured as a patriarchal system.

In conflict zones women have suffered many atrocities including sexual abuse such as rape, but it is only now that the voices of the survivors are being heard. The little space that has been opened up for women in peacekeeping discussions is not comparable to the atrocities committed against them. We celebrate women who have publicly raised issues of justice in local meetings and in various forums, seeking justice for survivors.

Women have dealt with issues of injustice affecting children. In the light of the effects of HIV/AIDS, many children in communities in East and Central Africa have been orphaned. As a result of attitudes to and lack of support for teenage parents and illegitimate children, many children are growing up on the streets. Their future is likely to be bleak and they could enter the cycle of poverty and be perpetrators of violence, as they are often targets for those who plan and execute violence. Women have set up various projects to cater for the basic needs of these children, seeking ways to get them off the streets and ways to break the cycle of poverty. These women's groups focus on dealing with people who are vulnerable in society. Their peace work does not depend on donor funding but on their own initiatives using available resources. Their form of engaging in peace is to empower those whom society has neglected or pushed to the margins, such as orphans, giving them an opportunity to learn skills of survival.

Women are still relegated to an inferior status in the economic, political, social, and religious spheres of society. The work of the USFW is important in peacebuilding. Their work in peacebuilding emanates from the knowledge that relationships are important because they hold society together. Their engagement with peacebuilding is at the level of social justice. The women do this because of their experience of injustice within the patriarchal system.

It seems to us that peacebuilding is never finished – peace is a process. It is a way of thinking, acting and being that characterises all of us at our best.

We pray that some of what we have said has spoken to you.

African peacemaker stories

While preparing this lecture Esther and Cécile spoke to a number of people engaged in peacebuilding in East and Central Africa. The following are their personal stories.

Hezron Masitsa

My name is Hezron Masitsa. I was born into a Quaker family and raised with grandparents who were among the first Quaker converts in western Kenya. From an early age my grandparents taught us values of respect, peace and truth and taught us not to do harm to anyone or any creature.

After high school I joined university and studied sociology. I completed my degree and was looking for a job. There was an opening to be a warden in a Quaker centre in Nairobi but I was not keen. One of the pastors challenged me to take up the job, saying that I had asked him to pray for a job but when a door opened I did not want that job. I took the job as a stop gap with the intention of moving on to a "bigger" job. I ended up working at the centre for nine years and through that entered peace work. At the centre I was exposed to Quaker teaching over and above what my grandparents had taught me. This included the knowledge that Quakers not only emphasise peace as one of the ideals but are also a peace church.

In 2002 I was sent to Cape Town in South Africa and went through training in the Alternatives to Violence Project. This training opened a whole new world for me in regard to peace and I got immersed in it. I was seeking more and wanting to share more on what it meant to be a peace church. Among the major aspects that caught me was the saying that there is "that of God in every person". I began my peace work at an interfaith level, bringing Christians and Muslims together. This had challenges because of the Christians being afraid of having Muslims among them. But it opened up space for Christians to speak about issues of peace.

My training in restorative justice added to my peace engagement as I was able to see how using restorative justice maintains relationships better than criminal justice. This for me became an avenue through which to begin to look into issues of social justice. One issue that was very close for me was seeing how my mother had been abused due to the injustices rooted in the patriarchal culture. My mother tried to fit into a patriarchal cultural system but failed. She was rejected when alive and rejected at death. After she died I had to argue with my uncles about where to bury her; the "crime" she had committed was not to stay within an abusive marriage. I realised that, even though Quakers were historically among the first people to open up space for women, in the Quaker meetings I attended women were still defined from the cultural perspective that they were not allowed into positions of leadership. Denying women space to exercise their gifts was and is a justice issue, and so, when one is dealing with peace and conflict issues, it should start from the relationship between men and women.

Another case was of a woman who was from a different ethnic community and married to my cousin. Her husband (my cousin) died of an HIV-related illness and when she came to bury him she was treated with animosity, including blame, stigma and discrimination on the basis of her ethnicity. My uncle was so angry with her that all he wanted was for her to declare the properties that his son held. This woman was not allowed to grieve for her husband, and no one cared that she had a young child. After the funeral she was taken to court to declare property. I was so saddened by this event that I approached my uncle to ask that the matter be removed from the court and handled within the family to restore some dignity to this woman and also to build relations with her as she had a son from my uncle's own son. My uncle listened to me and withdrew the case from court. The matter was discussed within the family and, even if this woman finally leaves the family, she will still be able to visit her son. This is an example of how widows suffer due to the social injustices rooted in a patriarchal culture.

Relationships between men and women should not be hierarchical in the sense of seeing one as a lesser human being than the other; instead, both men and women should be seen as people in whom God's spirit dwells, which in Quaker terminology is that of God in each person. The experiences of my mother and other family members increased my motivation for peace and encouraged me to see peacebuilding as a lifestyle and not a project that is undertaken just when there is conflict in a nation. National conflicts are a reflection of conflicts on the family level.

The Quaker church in Kenya has done many things but should lead by example on all issues, especially in the treatment of women.

David Niyonzima

My name is David Niyonzima. I am a pastor in Burundi Yearly Meeting and the founder of the non-governmental organisation Trauma Healing and Reconciliation Services (THARS).

I began working for peace after eight of my eleven students were killed in an attack on 25 October 1993. I realised that the only reason I survived the killing was because I was away from the scene talking to someone. I was convinced that God spared my life so that I may do all I can to plant the seed of peace so that what happened might not happen again. Since then, I have been combining peacebuilding and trauma-healing in an effort to establish lasting peace. The kind of peace work I am doing is that type of work that involves the community. I am working in Burundi in particular but also in the African Great Lakes region in general. I am using the Alternatives to Violence Project (AVP) as an approach because I found that it brings together the healing model, the prevention of violence and the transformation of the conflict.

I am currently working with communities in Burundi. The youth affiliated to political parties are becoming perpetrators of the violence that began in 2015 in response to political unrest surrounding pressure on the president to give up his candidacy for a third term in office. I am doing peace work with these youths, including community representatives at the grassroots level, through THARS. My colleagues and I are using the workshops and techniques that are provided in the AVP manuals as we have all been trained in how to use them.

One of our success stories is as follows. It all started with the beginning of the protests. During the protests, some youths affiliated with the opposition parties decided to search the houses that belonged to the families of *Imbonerakure** in an effort to find arms that might have been distributed to them. As a result three

---

* The *Imbonerakure* (the Kirundi word for "those that see far") is the youth wing of Burundi's ruling party, the National Council for the Defence of Democracy – Forces for the Defence of Democracy (CNDD-FDD). It was established to maintain security at a local level, but its influence and authority reportedly overrules that of the police force, allowing the group to commit acts of violence without fear of legal repercussions.

grenades were found and were given to the police. Because of this finding, the youth of the opposition destroyed some houses belonging to *Imbonerakure* families as well as the ruling party's centres almost across the whole area of Nyabiraba, a commune in rural Bujumbura. Also 870 t-shirts belonging to the ruling party (uniforms for the electoral campaign) were burnt by the youth of the opposition. The operation was considered by *Imbonerakure* as unacceptable aggression and they immediately prepared a punitive attack against the protesting youth. *Imbonerakure* got reinforcements of 70 other members of the ruling party from a neighbouring commune, known as Mutambu, and they attacked the youth of the opposition parties with sticks and stones. Many people were injured, and there was one death on the side of the *Imbonerakure*. Many youths on both sides were taken to hospital and many others fled their homes.

THARS intervened when another attack was being prepared between the two fiercely opposed groups. THARS got the news about this planned attack and decided to go there with the objective of defusing the tension and preventing the attack. After two consecutive AVP workshops in which a total of 40 participants from the two opposing groups took part, both *Imbonerakure* and the youth of the opposition political parties confirmed that the workshops had caused them to totally abandon the plan. They confessed that they had resolved to seek dialogue on the questions that divided them instead of fighting.

The representatives of the protestors said that even if the protests continued to put pressure on the president, they would not use violence because they now understood that it does not solve problems and aggravates things instead. Even the *Imbonerakure* representatives expressed their regret for launching the attack first and confirmed that they would not do it again. The members of THARS believe that even those who fled might be able to return.

A challenge that we face is that the political leaders, who could also benefit from these workshops, require financial stipends to attend that we cannot afford. We are further challenged by the fact that we would have wished to move from the grassroots level to reach the political leadership, which sometimes manipulates youth in the current situation.

The peace work we are doing is sustainable in the sense that the workshops we are doing are a form of training that will be duplicated by the trained ones. What makes these workshops sustainable is the fact that we move from basic training to advanced training, and the skills and life changes are lived out by the workshop attendees in their constituencies.

This work of peacebuilding in Burundi has been funded on and off by individuals and by small grants and voluntary services.

Sizeli Marcellin

My name is Sizeli Marcellin. I am a member of the Friends Church of Rwanda and president of the Peace Commission of Rwanda Yearly Meeting.

I came into peace work after the genocide against Tutsi. First of all, where there is no problem, there is no way to find solutions. After genocide, I found that we need peace rather than other things, and I found that we need most peace and peacebuilding in Rwanda and all over the world. My trigger came when I took refuge at Amahoro Stadium during the genocide. Tutsi were being killed by Hutu. I survived but my family, including my wife, parents and children, were killed. I arrived at the stadium by chance and saw how people were angry, traumatised, had no hope, and were looking only for revenge. I found some survivors who had suffered more than me, and I was pushed by another power to start telling people that we need peace and reconciliation.

After the genocide, because I was a member of the Friends Church (historically a peace church), I started within displaced camps making reconciliations among people and later worked closer to my church, teaching peace and reconciliation. One lady from Kenya came to visit us, and she encouraged us to focus on peace and reconciliation as a Quaker value. I became a peacemaker, a peacebuilder, teaching peace to various people even within my church and my yearly meeting, because people were having problems or accusing each other. I became the coordinator of Rwanda Friends Peace House, where most peace activities of Rwanda Yearly Meeting were coordinated. I reconciled people in conflict and I advocated for some in order to get back their houses, which had been taken by others after the genocide, because most survivors' houses were destroyed or burnt. My work was concentrated at Friends Peace House, and focused at the beginning on survivors, released prisoners, reintegration of released prisoners, women who had lost their husbands, children's experiences of genocide, and women whose husbands or children were in prison. I do my peace work with victims of the genocide against Tutsi and with communities, church leaders, survivors of genocide, released prisoners, and prisoners.

If you want to do something and are pushed by another power from inside, it is easy to succeed; if you have a gift for what you are doing and are called to do it, you make it work. Friends in Rwanda contributed to my peace work or my calling. As a coordinator of Friends Peace House, my calling was increased and I increased the amount of peacebuilding we could do. I use the AVP approach, transformative mediation and conflict resolution. Also, when I became a Gacaca judge, I learnt a lot about restorative justice and reconciliation.

I have lots of success stories, but let me give just a few. Firstly, one person was angry after the genocide; he wanted to get revenge against another person. I talked with this other person and brought him to see the survivor. Instead of enacting revenge, the survivor found that the other person had done good things for him during the genocide. He was only generalising without knowing the truth.

My second story is from when the Friends Church organised AVP training for the community leaders from Ngoma District. Afterwards, the vice mayor told us that AVP is a tremendous tool for good governance: "The skills we have now will help us to respond peacefully in a situation of violence. They will also help us leaders to treat peacefully those who come to us. We will be able to listen to them and understand them, and will be able to find ways to solve their problems. We are grateful for this important tool for peace."

AVP is also helping prisoners in Rwanda. Most of them say that they never before realised that there is an option to respond to violence with nonviolence. If they had benefitted from AVP before the genocide, they would not be in prison. They are promising to use AVP principles in prison and among their families as well as in their respective communities when out of prison.

Achieving sustainability in peace work is not easy, but we see sustainability here in Rwanda in the fact that we have many people engaged in peace work. We also mentor young people, and even our government has a peace and reconciliation unit. This shows peace is seen as desirable even by our government, and this is further evidence of the sustainability of our work. This means that we are supported and encouraged by the government. When we started peacemaking, it was under Rwanda Yearly Meeting, but now we have many independent peace organisations.

Eli Nahimana

My name is Eli Nahimana. I am a pastor in Burundi Yearly Meeting and a peacemaker. Since the civil war, which began on 21 October 1993, I have been working for GTZ (Deutsche Gesellschaft für Technische Zusammenarbeit / German Society for Technical Cooperation) in the field of bridge construction. During the civil war, I saw how many people were brutally killed, some burnt alive, others with knives by ordinary people. On the other side of the conflict, the military forces used weapons to kill civilians whom they had been called to protect.

The destruction did not stop at lives; community infrastructures, beginning with some bridges I built, were also destroyed. Houses, fields and the environment were not safe. Part of the population took the path of exile while other people became refugees in their own country. My home town, Kibimba, was affected very severely by this war, with the massacre of Kibimba school students. More than 150 Tutsi were killed including over 70 students on one side. On the other side a multitude of Hutu were massacred by the military forces.

This situation created a divide between Hutu and Tutsi from my locality. We had to intervene to restore the good relations that had previously characterised both Hutu and Tutsi of this locality. It was in this context that I contributed to the creation of the Kibimba Peace Committee (KPC) in 1994 to change the passivity of this community. I also worked with numerous other organisations, including Healing and Rebuilding Our Communities (HROC), Innovations in Peacemaking Burundi (IPB), and the Ministry for Peace and Reconciliation under the Cross (MIPAREC). Initially I worked as a volunteer in conflict management and mediation and as a counsellor. Today I am a full-time worker at MIPAREC and a part-time worker with HROC and IPB.

My greatest success is the founding of KPC in 1994. This approach has made a difference in communities. Today KPC has become a door through which to enter communities. Many local and international organisations are using this approach in their interventions in Burundi. Locally, MIPAREC intervenes through the peace committees. International organisations such as Care

International and ZOA are also using peace committees as a gateway to the community. Even though we succeeded with peace committees, we are still facing challenges:

- The conflict persists but in a different form. Previously there were ethnic problems; now the problems have become more political.
- There is another considerable challenge from poverty and the large number of jobless people, mainly young people.
- We must sustain this peacebuilding work in Burundi, through healing wounds from trauma and through building the capacity of communities to manage conflict nonviolently.
- As trauma is caused by conflict, we must teach communities good ways to deal with conflict, which makes our work sustainable.

Quaker peace organisations and Mennonite Central Committee sponsor this work through fundraising.

Joseph Mamai

My name is Joseph Mamai and I am from Kenya. For four consecutive elections – 1992, 1997, 2002, and 2007 – I was forced out of my home and lost property due to ethnic and land clashes. It was only in 2013 that I was not forced out of my home. This was due to the peace work I was engaged in and how I had worked to help people stay at peace with each other.

The reasons for this conflict were tribal animosities, which were historically as a result of land demarcations and leadership roles among the tribes, which had been divided into political units of administration that appeared to suit the majority tribes. These boundaries started with the divisions of the colonial government. The minority tribes felt that they lacked positions of leadership and suffered when it came to sharing resources. The majority tribes did not like listening to the minority tribes, even when these tribes were putting forward a genuine case.

In the earlier days people fought with crude weapons such as bows, arrows and machetes. But in the 2007–8 post-election violence, guns were introduced, leading to worse outcomes than the earlier fights. In the earlier fights the conflicts took only two weeks but in 2007–8 they took over two months. In the earlier conflicts, my family and I sought a safe place to stay, but at the time of the 2007–8 violence I was the presiding clerk of Friends Church Peace Teams and together with other Quaker leaders we had to do something.

We came together and asked ourselves what we could do as a peace church. The first thing we did was to attend to the physical needs of the people affected before we began looking into other needs. After dealing with the physical needs, we knew that these people could not live in tents; they had to return to their homes – but their homes had been destroyed. The government decreed that all the people should return to their farms. But listening to the people in the camps, I learnt that they were not ready to return and the others in the villages were not ready to receive them.

One of the issues was the new identities that people had acquired – namely, "perpetrators" and "victims". This language was intimidating and was creating more animosity between the two groups, so we chose new words. We called those who had done the evicting the "receiving group" and those who had been evicted the "returning people". We set a day to meet the people in each of the camps and together discussed the mode of returning and the ways in which the returning group would be received. After days of discussion the two groups agreed that the evictees would return and be received. The receiving group accommodated the returnees and helped them to rebuild their houses.

Solange Maniraguha

My name is Solange Maniraguha. I am a member of Rwanda Yearly Meeting, a peacemaker and a facilitator for Healing and Rebuilding Our Communities (HROC).

I got into peace work after receiving and feeling peace inside me, after a long period of inner pain, lack of peace and frustration. The kind of peace work I am doing is to help people in their journeys of healing from their trauma and to help them rebuild themselves. I am doing this work in Rwanda, in various communities, through the HROC programme. I do my work through workshops on trauma-healing. The tools I like to use are many, among them the training manual on trauma counselling (HROC has a manual that it uses for different levels of people).

Concerning HROC's achievements there are many success stories I could share. Firstly, HROC helped me to heal my heart's wounds. It is not easy for a broken-hearted healer to listen to someone who is traumatised. But what I like about HROC is that it is helping people to discover themselves, to recognise their wickedness and trauma, to rehabilitate themselves, and then try to help those who are in need of healing. In addition, HROC helps to heal wounded hearts, encouraging people to forgive each other and then be reconciled. For example, in the community of Gisenyi, two families reconciled successfully. One survivor and a released prisoner who attended HROC training decided to forgive each other and their families became real friends. They are helping more people in forgiveness and reconciliation.

Trauma-healing is used to help people to recognise the signs of trauma and what they can do to help someone who is traumatised. It is also about helping people to see what they can do to avoid a second trauma. It is also about helping the supporting group to share their pain and sorrow and to seek advice and healing from their peers. Very serious cases are referred to a specialist, where people can get appropriate support to address their needs.

A challenging aspect of the peace work that I am doing is the fact that we have insufficient funds to reach all the communities we would like to reach. The same goes for doing follow-up work with the people we have trained, to see whether change is happening and what support and other resources the trainees need to sustain their peace work. We would like to empower the facilitators and healing companions to give assistance to people who are re-experiencing trauma, such as taking them to the hospital and following up on them.

This work is sustainable because people who have been trained are able to use the skills in their respective communities. This work is being funded mostly by the African Great Lakes Initiative in collaboration with Rwanda Yearly Meeting.

Levi Ndikumana

My name is Levi Ndikumana. I was born in Burundi and I am a member of Burundi Yearly Meeting.

Burundi has been ravaged by violent ethnic conflict since 1993. There were two options for young people: join the armed groups or go for peacebuilding. Since then, MIPAREC has contributed to peacebuilding by equipping young people with conflict management and mediation skills. Many peace committees have been born, and they have been able to mediate within communities. They have successfully brought together people from different ethnic groups using the tools of conflict management and mediation.

I have attended a three-month training course in Johannesburg on conflict transformation with the Coalition for Peace in Africa. I have also done other training such as conflict transformation in an armed context in Germany, then demobilisation, disarmament and reintegration training in the Netherlands. Over my 20 years in peacemaking, I have worked with communities by creating peace committees in Burundi, Rwanda and other parts of Africa. Today, I am still empowering the peace committees to have a positive impact in Burundi communities.

I also worked with government in the context of election monitoring and observation. For this reason I was chosen to be member of the national electoral commission in Burundi from 2005 to 2010. I have been part of the team of election observers in other countries too, such as Democratic Republic of Congo, Kenya, Rwanda, and South Sudan.

I am a member of Action for Conflict Transformation, a global movement for peace. We have been supported in our peace work by Mennonite Central Committee and Quaker Service Norway, the latter of which supported us through the Change Agents for Peace International programme. Sometimes I volunteer and sometimes I am invited or nominated to do my peace work.

In this work of peacebuilding, the foundation of MIPAREC is the contribution to peace in Burundi of which I am most proud. In addition, I have experienced success with the foundation of the Great Lakes Peacebuilding Institute and the peace clubs I am working with, which are contributing to peace and security in their respective communities as local peace initiatives.

We remain challenged by the persistence of conflict and poverty in Burundi. To make our peace work sustainable, we need to work from the grass roots and across faiths for peace.

Levi Munyemana

My name is Levi Munyemana. I am from Democratic Republic of Congo (DRC) and a member of the Evangelical Friends Church of Congo.

Our Great Lakes region is well known for its instability and refugees, as well as for the fact that it contains many people temporarily displaced across various countries. The lack of rule of law and respect for human rights were the origin of most of the conflicts that have ravaged the region.

In 1999 the Evangelical Friends Church of Rwanda invited me in. I took part in a workshop in conflict resolution, from which I obtained the light and skills to start doing something for peace in my community. The first target groups were community leaders, church leaders and young people. It was imperative to mix people from different ethnic groups and regions. With young people and women, we formed peace committees to ensure these people are helping in conflict resolution among their respective churches and communities.

Our work focused on Masisi in North Kivu Province, which is known worldwide as the cradle of the conflict in DRC. We work with key people, leaders of ethnic groups, youth, women, and religious leaders. Most of the time we use mediation as a tool.

Our work in bringing together people from different tribes and ethnic groups is very successful. We have had successes in North Kivu in bringing together Hunde and Lega, who for many years were enemies, divided and engaged in violent conflict. We organised platforms for dialogue, and the groups came together, forgave each other and are now coexisting peacefully. Then we started forming peace committees. The provincial government heard about this success and asked our permission to copy and utilise this approach. We are proud of this.

Something that makes our work sustainable is that the peace committees are contributing to our monthly activities, giving their time and their money. One of our donors is Quaker Service Norway; others are some international non-governmental organisations based in Goma, DRC.